The Atlantic

The Atlantic stretches from the icy coast of Greenland down through the tropics to Antarctica. It touches the shores of industrial North America and surrounds tiny, volcanic islands lost in the middle of the Ocean. With the aid of over fifty pictures, this book describes the peoples of the Atlantic, the great diversity of plants, animals and other creatures which live in its waters and on its shores, and the way we are exploiting oil and mineral resources on and below the sea floor. You will discover, too, about tides and currents, and follow the historic trade routes between North America and Europe. The Atlantic has always held a fascination for explorers – the Celts, the Vikings, and of course Christopher Columbus and his followers. You should find plenty to satisfy your own sense of adventure. There is a glossary and a list of books to read at the back of the book.

SEAS AND OCEANS

The Atlantic

Edited by Pat Hargreaves

WAYLAND

SILVER BURDETT

© Copyright 1980 Wayland Publishers Ltd
First published in 1980 by
Wayland (Publishers) Limited
61 Western Road, Hove,
East Sussex BN3 1JD, England

Published in the United States by
Silver Burdett Press
Morristown, New Jersey
1987 printing

Phototypeset by
Trident Graphics Limited, Reigate, Surrey
Printed in Italy by
G. Canale & C. S.p.A., Turin

Library of Congress Cataloging-in-Publication Data

The Atlantic.

(Seas and oceans)
Includes index.
Summary: Describes the Atlantic Ocean, its tides and currents,
exploration and trade routes, islands and ports, plants and animals, and
oil and mineral resources.
1. Atlantic Ocean–Juvenile literature. [1. Atlantic Ocean. 2. Ocean]
I. Hargreaves, Pat. II. Series.
[GC481.A84 1986] 551.46'1 86-29852
ISBN 0-382-06466-6 (Silver Burdett)

Seas and Oceans

Three-quarters of the earth's surface is covered by sea. Each book in this series takes you on a cruise of a mighty ocean, telling you of its history, discovery and exploration, the people who live on its shores, and the animals and plants found in and around it.

The Atlantic
The Caribbean and Gulf of Mexico
The Mediterranean
The Antarctic
The Arctic
The Indian Ocean
The Red Sea and Persian Gulf
The Pacific

Contents

1 A GREAT OCEAN

In this book you will learn all kinds of fascinating facts about the Atlantic Ocean. It is not the biggest ocean in the world, but in some ways it is the most important. It carries the largest amount of shipping of any ocean, most of which travels between the highly industrial countries of North America and Europe. It is also one of the most widely explored oceans in the world. This is particularly true of the North Atlantic.

The Atlantic Ocean extends from Greenland and Iceland in the north, across the equator to Antarctica in the south. In the old days, when sailing ships travelled round the world to trade, sailors would find themselves moving in the space of a few weeks from the cold of the Antarctic, through warmer waters to the heat of the tropics, and back to the cool climate of Europe. (These days, yachtsmen do the journey for pleasure!) There are icebergs floating in the ocean near Greenland and Antarctica. In the tropics, on the other hand, the waters are very warm, so you could swim all day without getting cold.

The Atlantic joins the Indian Ocean south of Africa. Further south it merges with the Antarctic Ocean. North and South America lie to the west, Antarctica to the south, Africa and Europe to the east and Greenland and Iceland to the north. The Atlantic is connected to the other oceans by fairly narrow passages. One of

Left Children playing in boats among ice floes at Kap Dan, Killusah Island, Greenland – just below the Arctic Circle.

these is Drake Passage between South America and Antarctica, which connects the Atlantic and Pacific Oceans. It was discovered accidentally by Sir Francis Drake when his ship was blown from the west coast of South America round Cape Horn to the east coast during a gale. However, since the Panama Canal was built across Central America in 1914, few ships now take the long southern route round Cape Horn.

Many different peoples live around the Atlantic, and the ocean is important to all of them, though in different ways. First of all, it helps control the temperature of the land. When the wind blows over a long stretch of sea, the air is warmed or cooled to nearly the same temperature as the sea itself. In western Europe, the prevailing winds are from the south-west. They pass over fairly warm water before reaching the land and so the climate of western Europe is mild. In eastern North America, prevailing winds in winter blow from the cold Arctic area of northern Canada and so provide a much colder climate than in western Europe.

Much of our food comes from the seas. Fishing is important to many countries, and various kinds of fish are found in different parts of the Atlantic.

Minerals also come from the ocean or, more accurately, from the earth underneath the ocean (though there are small quantities of various minerals and important chemicals present in sea-water). There are especially rich

deposits of minerals, such as oil and phosphates, on the continental shelves (the shallow water areas at the edge of the ocean). Phosphates are used to make fertilizers. There are large continental shelves next to many countries. These include Ireland, Britain, France, and many African countries, Argentina and Brazil in South America, and the United States of America and Canada. Most of these countries are now exploring their continental shelves in search of the mineral riches they may contain.

The Atlantic Ocean also provides an important means of transport. Ships can cross it easily, and can carry large loads more cheaply than aircraft. Modern ships can cross from North America to Europe in less than a week. Grain, sugar, fruit, chemicals, cars and lorries, and many other raw materials and manufactured goods are transported to and from various countries every year.

Right A woman inspects the fishing catch on a deserted, unspoilt beach in Sierra Leone, West Africa.

Overleaf Map of Atlantic Ocean.

GREENLAND

EUROPE

A F R I C A

NORTH
AMERICA

New York

Azores

Canary Islands

Cape Verde Islands

M I D - A T L A N

SOUTH AMERICA

St Helena

G

E

ANTARCTICA

Buenos Aires

Drake Passage

2 THE MOVING CONTINENTS

Continental drift, volcanoes and earthquakes

If you look at a map of the whole Atlantic Ocean, you may notice that the coasts of North and South America have a similar shape to those of Europe and Africa. If you could move the continents together, they look as though they would fit neatly against each other. The east coast of North America would fit Europe and the round bulge of North Africa, and South America would lie snugly against the rest of Africa. The reason for this is that once, many millions of years ago, these lands really were joined together! Animals could move freely between Europe and North America, and between South America and Africa. We can find their remains, called fossils, preserved in rocks on both sides of the Atlantic as proof of this.

About 180 million years ago, the great continent in the north, called Laurentia, began to break up. Cracks formed in the ground, and molten rock, or lava, began to pour out and form volcanoes. Gradually, over millions of years, the two sides moved apart, the cracks widened, and the ground in between them filled

Right See how the continents have changed their shape over millions of years.

Opposite The Atlantic sea-bed showing the Mid-Atlantic Ridge. If the ocean were drained of water, this is what it would look like.

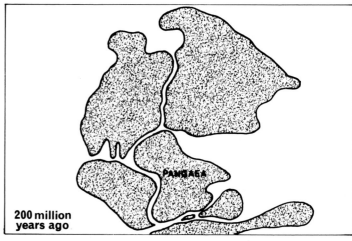
200 million years ago

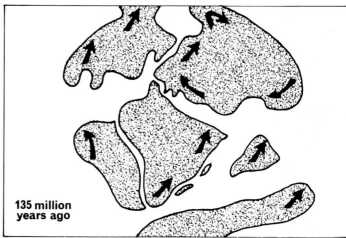
135 million years ago

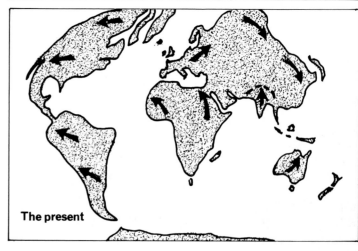
The present

up with lava and sank, until at last it was below sea-level and the water poured in. But the sides – the Continents of North America and Europe – continued to separate, and the ground in between, which was now beneath water, continued to sink until it was several kilometres below sea-level. The volcanoes sank with it and they eventually made up an enormous range of underwater mountains in the centre of the ocean. This is now called the Mid-Atlantic Ridge.

Some time later, about 130 million years ago, the southern super-continent began to break up, and South America and Africa separated to form the South Atlantic. But continental drift, as this movement is called, has not yet stopped. The continents are still moving apart today, at speeds of about two centimetres a year in the North Atlantic, and three centimetres a year in the South Atlantic.

Along the centre of the Mid-Atlantic Ridge, the sea floor is still cracking and moving apart. The cracking of the rocks causes the Earth to shake, producing earthquakes. Some islands, like the Azores, are very close to this movement of the Mid-Atlantic Ridge, and from time to time they are shaken by earthquakes.

As the rocks break and separate, lava wells up from inside the earth to fill the cracks. It is this lava which makes up the new sea floor as the sides move apart. It also forms new underwater volcanoes along the centre line The old volcanoes gradually move away on either side as the sea floor continues to separate. You will see from this that the sea floor gets older the further it is from the centre of the Mid-Atlantic Ridge. The very youngest rocks, formed from the most recent eruptions, are at the centre. The oldest ones, which formed when the continents first began to split up, are at the sides near the land. As the sea floor gets older, it gradually sinks, so the ocean is always shallower in the middle, over the crest of the Mid-Atlantic Ridge.

Left A spectacular, bird's eye view of a volcanic eruption on the island of Heimaey, near Iceland. Volcanoes occur on the sea floor too.

Rocks and sediments

The continents are continuously being eroded by the weather. In winter, or on high mountains, frost cracks rocks and breaks them up into boulders. These are gradually ground down into smaller pebbles, gravel, sand and silt (fine mud-like particles), and washed down to the sea. They then mount up as sediments on top of the rocks of the sea floor. Most of the sedimentary particles fall near the continents, but some of the smallest particles can drift right out to the middle of the ocean. These sediments are gradually pressed down by their own weight and eventually turn into hard rocks. The rocks made up of the finest particles are called clays; others are shales and sandstones.

When tiny plants and animals living in the sea die, their bodies fall down on to the sea floor and become incorporated in the sediments. When they first fall to the sea floor such sediments are like soft mud. They are called 'oozes'. They gradually harden to form rocks such as chalk and limestone.

The remains of the larger animals, such as

Below Limestone rock which contains the fossils of many sea creatures.

Right Scientists examine sediment and rock hauled up from the sea-bed.

16

the skeletons of fishes, and shells of shellfish, also fall to the bottom of the sea and become part of the sediments. They may be preserved as fossils.

In some oceans (though not the Atlantic at present) the continents move towards each other instead of drifting apart, and then the sediments and rocks between them may be squeezed together and pushed up out of the sea. Some of the rocks now found on land were formed in this way, and they contain fossils of the shellfish and other animals which dropped into them millions of years ago. If you look in the right rocks, especially limestones and shales, you may find the fossil remains of some of these ancient sea creatures.

3 EARLY EXPLORERS OF THE ATLANTIC

Ancient peoples

Perhaps one of the most significant events in history was the discovery of America in 1492 by Columbus – but he was not the first European to cross the Atlantic. Little is known of the explorers of ancient times, but in about 320 B.C. a man named Pytheas from Marseilles, in the south of France, made a voyage, apparently to find the source of the tin brought by Phoenician traders from Cornwall to the Mediterranean. He sailed round the British Isles and found a far northern land, possibly Iceland.

The Atlantic may have been crossed in the early centuries of our history by the Romans in their galleys (types of boat) or by Irish monks. Recently, an expedition was made in a traditional Irish *curragh*, a boat made from skins, to show that the trans-Atlantic crossing, such as

Below 1,400 years after St Brendan's legendary Atlantic crossing in a leather boat, four men re-enact the hazardous, 4,000-mile journey.

Above The discovery of Greenland by Eric the Red in the year 983.

that possibly described in the legend of St Brendan (an Irish abbot living in the sixth century A.D.) could have been made in such a craft.

Irish monks certainly sailed great distances in search of lonely islands where they could establish their monasteries. When the Vikings discovered Iceland, in the ninth century A.D., there were Irish settlers there. A hundred years later, a Viking ship, blown off course, reached Greenland. It was from there that in about the year A.D. 1000 the Vikings sailed for America, but they established no permanent colonies there. As the climate worsened during the later Middle Ages, the Greenland settlement also disappeared. Memories of these adventurous explorations faded, and for many years the stories of discoveries in the west told in the Icelandic sagas (epic poems which date from the eleventh to the thirteenth centuries) were thought to be mere inventions. It was not until the fifteenth century, when European nations to the south became interested in extending trade and alliances with other peoples through voyages of discovery, that modern knowledge of the Atlantic began.

Later explorations

Above Prince Henry the Navigator of Portugal planning his Captains' voyages from his castle near Cape St Vincent.

The great age of European discovery began in the fifteenth century, when a Portuguese prince, known as Henry the Navigator, began sending expeditions southwards along the African coast. This led eventually to the rounding of the Cape of Good Hope by Bartholomew Diaz and to Vasco da Gama's arrival in India in 1498.

Meanwhile, western geographers knew from the travels of Marco Polo in the thirteenth century, of the existence of Cathay (China) and of the island of Japan. Christopher Columbus, an Italian from Genoa who arrived in Portugal after being shipwrecked off its shores, suggested that rather than travel eastwards from Europe to the Far East, it would be quicker to sail westwards. However, he did not realize just how large the continent of Asia was, and he also thought that the circumference of the earth (that is the distance round it) was smaller than it really was.

Henry the Navigator had already sent expeditions to the west, but they had discovered only small island groups, like the Azores, and were beaten back by westerly winds. Having failed to arouse interest in his ideas in Portugal, Columbus went to Spain and persuaded the King and Queen to support his venture to travel west.

Columbus expected to be able to sail straight across the Atlantic to the Far East. His ships were assisted by the north-east trade winds, and in October 1492, instead of arriving in China or Japan, he saw part of the New World –

a small island in the Bahamas. During this and several further voyages, Columbus explored the coasts and islands of the Caribbean Sea. It was left to his followers to explore and name the new continent of America. Columbus never did reach the Far East.

Below One of Columbus's ships, *Santa Maria*, was wrecked on the coast of Hispaniola on Christmas Eve, 1492.

Right A French sixteenth-century map of the world, drawn specially for seafarers. On such charts the lettering and illustration in the northern hemisphere were often put in upside down.

4 THE MOVING WATER

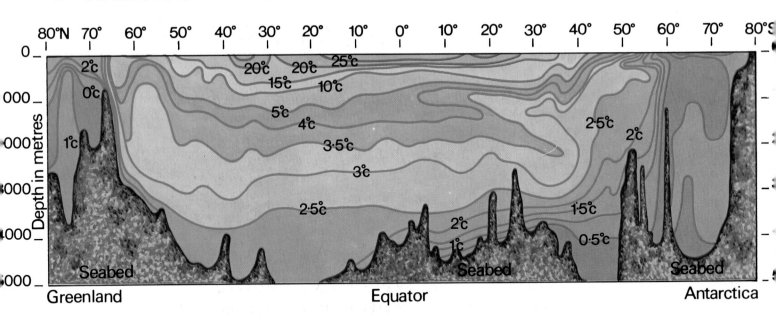

Above A cross-section of the Atlantic Ocean from the surface to the sea-bed between Greenland and Antarctica. The temperature at the surface at the equator is about 25°C. Near the sea-bed it is only 2.5°C or less.

Heat and salt

The Atlantic Ocean stretches from the cold northern waters around Iceland, Norway and Greenland, through the hot tropical and equatorial area between Africa and South America to the stormy seas that surround the Antarctic continent. The differences in climate between these areas account for the fact that the waters of the Atlantic vary in temperature and saltiness (or salinity as it is known).

In the Arctic and Antarctic areas, the severe cold in winter makes the surface water dense (heavy) and it sinks to the sea-bed. This surface water is replaced by warmer water from surrounding areas, which in turn sinks down as it gets colder. The cold water then spreads very slowly towards the equator

underneath the warm layers which are heated by the sun. The cold water fills nearly all of the ocean below the surface so that even at the equator, where the surface water is hotter than a good summer day in Britain, the water approximately one kilometre (half a mile) down is very cool and the water at the bottom (at five kilometres or three miles) is as cold as a cold British winter day. The temperature on the surface of the water, in all but the tropical regions, changes with the seasons. The summer sun warms the surface layers and makes them less dense so they stay at the top, but the

24

winter storms cool this surface water and mix it with the colder layers below.

The amount of salt in the water changes a little according to the depth of the water and its distance from the Poles. In the far north and south, and near the sea-bed, sea-water has a salinity of about 35 grammes (1.2 oz.) of salt to 1000 grammes (35.2 oz.) of water (that is the same as dissolving about two level tablespoons of salt in half a litre – about a pint – of water). The highest salinities are near the surface at about 30° north and 30° south of the equator. This is because these areas are very hot and get very little rain, so the sea-water evaporates and is more salty. Even here, however, there is still only 36 grammes of salt to 1000 grammes of water. So the variation in salinity is very slight.

Above A special meter which is used to measure the saltiness, temperature and depth of sea-water.

Currents

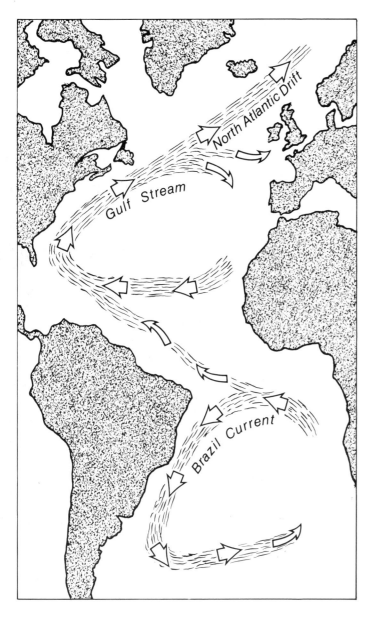

Above The main currents in the Atlantic are the Brazil Current, the Gulf Stream and the North Atlantic Drift.

The water of the ocean moves slowly near the sea-bed and faster at the surface. These movements of water are called currents. Some of these currents, where they are strong enough, are given names. The best known is the Gulf Stream, which flows northward along the coast of the United States, past Canada and Newfoundland and across the ocean bringing warm water all the way to the British Isles.

At the beginning, off the coast of Florida, the Gulf Stream is narrow and fast-flowing (about nine kilometres or four miles an hour). It becomes broader and slower as it meanders to the north. Why should the Gulf Stream be so strong? Why is it where it is? It is partly because of the spinning of the earth and partly because of the pattern of winds over the ocean that the strongest currents (like the Gulf Stream) are found on the western side of all the oceans. In the South Atlantic there is a current like the Gulf Stream but not as strong, again on the western side, flowing towards the south. This is known as the Brazil Current.

The Gulf Stream can be recognized not just by its fast flow but by the change in temperature as it is crossed. To the south of the current the water is warm, and to the north it becomes colder. Seamen can tell whether they are north or south of the current by feeling how warm the water is. This technique has been used for many years by the captains of sailing ships to help them find the best position for the current to help them along.

This difference in temperature makes the weather foggy off Newfoundland, where the warm winds from south of the Gulf Stream blow over cold water to the north. This is near where the ocean liner, the *Titanic*, sank in 1912 after hitting an iceberg in the fog.

Above The *Titanic* plunging beneath the waves off Newfoundland. Many of the passengers and crew went to an icy grave.

Left An instrument used to measure the movement of currents.

5 WAVES AND TIDES

Waves

Waves at sea are caused by the wind blowing over the water. At first it ruffles the water a little, but if very strong winds blow for half a day or longer, they can produce waves 20 or even 30 metres (70 to 100 ft) high. That is four or five times as high as an ordinary two-storey house. Imagine yourself in a ship floating in the trough (the lowest part) of one of these huge waves with a crest 25 metres (80 ft) high, only 150 metres (500 ft) away, roaring towards you at 50 or 60 kilometres (30 or 40 miles) per hour, and you will begin to realize how alarmed sailors must be when they are caught in a storm!

The north-east Atlantic Ocean off the British Isles and France is one of the stormiest oceans in the world. In any year, the total amount of energy in the waves arriving on the western shores of the United Kingdom and Ireland is about four times as much as all the electrical energy used in the United Kingdom during that year. It would be of great benefit if only a part of this energy could be used, because it is free, it will never be exhausted, and it does not

Below Stormy waves breaking on the Atlantic coast of Ireland.

Above Artist's impression of the Salter Duck in operation.

cause any pollution. There are devices, such as the 'Salter Duck' and the 'Cockerell Raft', which are now being tested and which could extract this energy, but the problems of doing so on a large scale would be great.

Waves cause a lot of damage because they can sink quite large ships, destroy sea walls, and damage oil platforms. Because of this, we need to understand how waves behave and so help to reduce both the losses and the cost. It is difficult to measure waves accurately because they are complicated in shape and are continually moving, but developments in electronics have helped scientists to build reliable recording instruments. They are installed in Ocean Weather Ships or Light Vessels and small floating buoys, and measure the waves several times every day.

Above Children scurry for safety after watching a schooner at Boston being demolished by heavy seas caused by Hurricane Donna.

Tides

Anyone who has spent a day by the sea will know the slow, regular, in-and-out movements of the water which we call tides. As the water returns from its lowest level it destroys sand castles. As it gradually floods the sea shore it fills rock pools, which are the homes of some plants and animals.

Around the Atlantic one complete 'in-out-in' tidal cycle takes on average 12 hours 26 minutes. Although ancient people knew that tides were related to the movements of the Moon and the Sun, it was the British physicist Isaac Newton (1642–1727) who first explained how they are formed by 'gravitational forces'.

Below Ocean tides are caused by the gravitational pull of the Sun and the Moon.

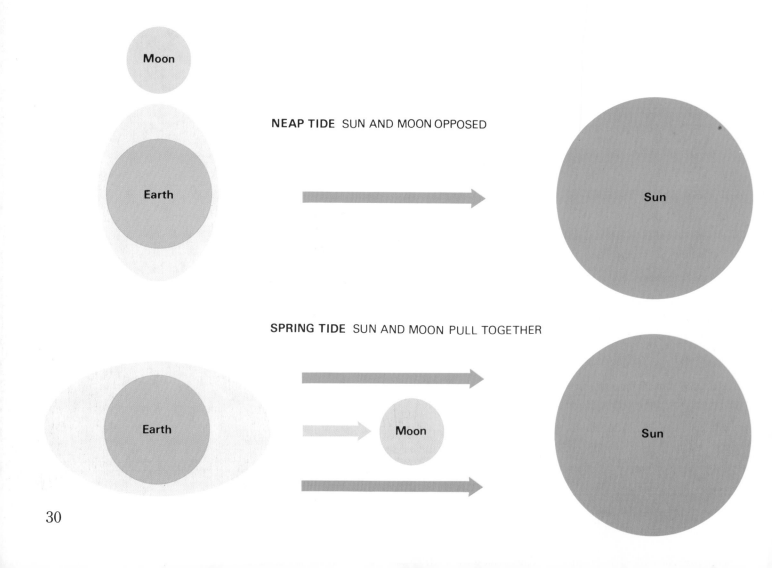

NEAP TIDE SUN AND MOON OPPOSED

Moon

Earth

Sun

SPRING TIDE SUN AND MOON PULL TOGETHER

Earth

Moon

Sun

Above Evening tide – a wave breaks on a rocky shore.

As the Moon and Earth circle each other every month, the gravitational pull between them just balances their tendency to fly apart. On the side of the Earth nearer the Moon, the larger gravitational pull produces a bulge of water. This is balanced by the force of the Earth's spin throwing the water on the opposite side of the Earth away from the Moon, producing a second bulge. The Earth rotates once a day giving each point two high tides as it passes through the two bulges. Because the bulges rotate slowly with the Moon, it takes 24 hours 52 minutes for two of these cycles to be completed.

The Moon's tides in the Atlantic are about three times bigger than the Sun's tides, which work in the same way as the Moon's tides. At new and full Moon, the Sun and Moon act together to give large spring tides every fourteen days. When they pull in opposition to each other, small 'neap' tides occur.

The tides spread as waves from the ocean on to the shallower continental shelves. The height increases from less than one metre (just over 3 ft) to more than fifteen metres (50 ft) in the Bay of Fundy, the Bristol Channel and the Gulf of St Malo. The first scheme to use tidal (rather than wave) energy is at La Rance in France. Here water trapped behind the barrage at high tide turns turbines to make electricity as it flows out at low tide.

Right A sandy beach at low tide. The movement of the water sculpts the sand into ridges.

6 PLANTS AND ANIMALS OF THE OPEN SEA

Life near the surface

In the open Atlantic Ocean, forms of marine life include not only large whales, smaller dolphins, turtles, fish, crustaceans, squid and jellyfish, but also millions of very small plants and animals of many different kinds, which drift with the sea-water. They are called plankton.

If we were to go far out over the deep sea in a boat and look down at the water we might catch a glimpse of a few larger fish, but it would be difficult to see the camouflaged plankton which live both on the surface and deeper down.

In the surface layers of the sea there is sunlight. Nearer the sea floor it is very dark. First of all let us look at the tiny plankton in the surface zone. Floating here are many microscopic plants called phytoplankton. If there are enough of these tiny plants they can make the sea look green. They are very important, because they form the harvest of the sea. They are able, in the presence of sunlight, to renew themselves – that is to keep on growing. For this they need carbon dioxide, water and various nutrients that are present in the sea. Many of the planktonic animals (called zooplankton) feed on the phytoplankton, and they in turn are eaten by larger animals. This process is called a 'food chain'. For instance,

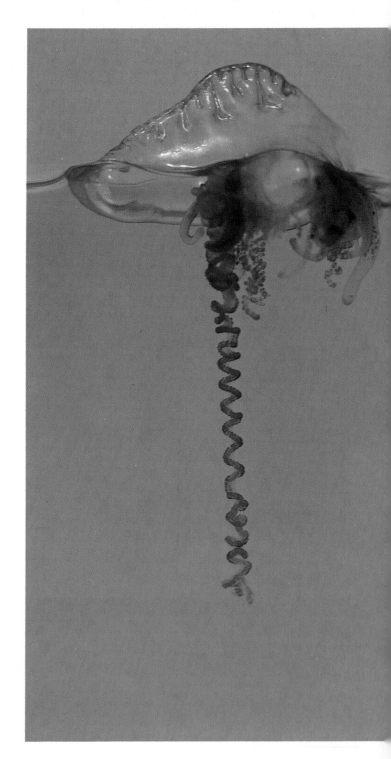

Right The Portuguese man-of-war is a colony of small creatures held on the water surface by a gas-filled float. The long tentacles sting and are used to catch prey.

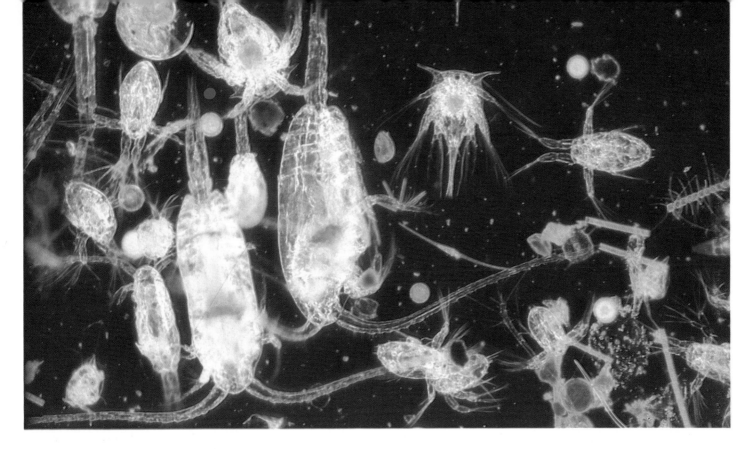

some types of shrimp feed on phytoplankton and these shrimps are eaten by some whales.

The small planktonic animals in the upper layers of the sea are very beautiful. There are tiny fish, crustaceans, molluscs, arrow worms, larval forms of many different types such as barnacles, and others. Most are light in colour, often blue or silver, and therefore not seen easily in the blue-green sunlit sea. This helps to camouflage (or hide) them from other animals which could eat them. Like the plants, the animals weigh little and float easily if they are very small. Some have special structures for staying afloat. The Portuguese man-of-war has a gas-filled 'float'. The by-the-wind sailor has a float and a 'sail' and so it can be pushed along by the wind or by currents.

Above Some of the many types of plankton found in surface waters.

Below Another type of plankton. Beneath the float are tentacles, a mouth and reproduction organs.

Life in deeper waters

Sunlight cannot penetrate far into the deep water. At depths from 200 metres to about 800 metres (656 to 2,624 ft) the water is only dimly lit – a twilight zone where plants cannot grow. Below this there is inky blackness right down to the sea floor.

Throughout the water there are drifting planktonic animals, most less than one centimetre (half an inch) long. Many are related to the surface types but often the deeper forms are darker and coloured black, red, brown or purple. Large squid and fish are also found, some with powerful bodies adapted for catching prey. Many of the animals in the twilight zone move upwards towards the surface layers each evening at dusk to feed. Here they remain throughout the night. At dawn the next day they sink to the depths. However, not all animals do this. Some remain in very deep water for most of their lives and eat other

Below A squid from the deeper waters of the ocean. It is covered in 'jewels' – tiny patches of light produced by chemicals in its body.

Above A type of angler fish with a lure to catch prey.

Left The bass has a streamlined body. It feeds on other fish, squid and crustaceans.

animals or the remains of dead creatures which fall from the layers above.

Imagine a journey to the depths. What might we see? The animals of the deep, although beautiful in shape and colour, would look dark and shadowy in the dim light. However, many would have fantastic luminous, blue-green patterns of dots or lines, and sometimes patches of light. These are produced by chemicals in the animals' bodies. (Glow worms, which you can see on land, give off light in a similar way.)

The whole effect would be that of a dark night sky full of tiny moving jewels. If we were to play a spotlight on the animals we would see how cleverly their bodies are adapted to their way of life. The purple, red and cream jellyfish have long tentacles for trapping food; the black, carnivorous fish have large teeth and jaws; and the angler fish has a 'fishing line' lit up at the end to lure prey.

Life on the sea floor

The large attached seaweeds which can be seen on any rocky shore extend into the water below the tidemarks, but only down to 50 metres (164 ft). Beyond this, the water is deep and on the sea floor there is insufficient sunlight to allow the plants to grow. So the sea floor is populated entirely by animals. Although the sea-floor animals become fewer as the depth increases, some are found even in the deepest parts of the ocean which, in the Atlantic, means 10,000 metres (33,000 ft) below the surface. Here it is dark and the water temperature is close to freezing.

In the more shallow regions close to the shore, the type of sea floor is very variable. There are rocks, boulders, sand and gravel. In the deeper parts of the ocean the sea floor is covered by a thick layer of fine mud formed of the chalky or glass-like skeletons of millions and millions of tiny planktonic animals which sank to the bottom when they died.

Living on the sea floor in shallower water are animals ranging from tiny, single-celled creatures like amoeba to the large fishes. Sponges, corals and sea anemones are firmly attached to the bottom, just like plants. These fixed animals have to feed. They cannot hunt for food, and so depend on water currents bringing it to them in the form of plankton or the remains of dead animals. Many other creatures, such as crabs and lobsters, starfishes and sea-urchins, and many molluscs, crawl slowly across the sea floor picking up pieces of food as they go.

Beneath the sediment surface, yet another world exists. Here living animals can be found buried. Some feed by swallowing the mud for the tiny food particles which it contains. Others filter water through special tubes which stick up through the mud surface.

Above The sun starfish can be up to 26cm across. It feeds on animals including other starfish.

Opposite A common prawn moving slowly through seaweed on the sea floor.

7 THE LONG JOURNEY

Migration and fish

Planktonic animals including fish larvae drift along passively with the water currents. Larger animals too may drift, but often they are strong enough to swim against the currents. Some fish migrate over long distances in search of food, for breeding or sometimes because of climatic conditions. Scientists are still not sure about the migration patterns of many fish. One method of finding out is to tag the fish and then release them into the sea.

Some are recaptured days or months later. The scientist can then tell how far they have travelled from the point from which they were released. Some commercially important fish, such as salmon, migrate. They remain in the sea for much of their adult life but return to rivers to spawn.

One of the most interesting migration patterns is that of the eel. In the Atlantic there are two types of eel: the North American and the European. Near the centre of the Atlantic is the Sargasso Sea, a region where there is a

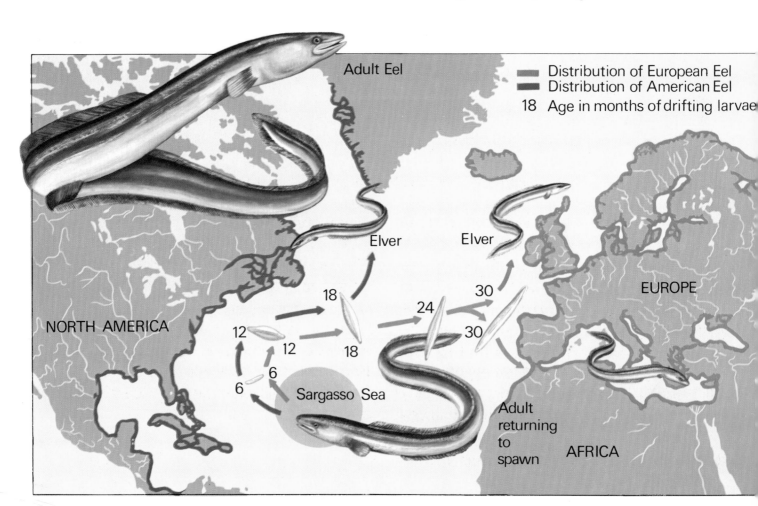

Adult Eel

Elver   Elver

— Distribution of European Eel
— Distribution of American Eel
18 Age in months of drifting larvae

EUROPE

NORTH AMERICA

18   24   30
12   30
12   18
6
6   Sargasso Sea

Adult
returning
to
spawn   AFRICA

Above Adult common eels among seaweed. Males grow to about 50cm, which is half the size of females.

special kind of large, floating seaweed. Here in the summer, tiny eel larvae called *leptocephali* hatch out. They are less than one centimetre (half an inch) long, transparent and slender. They drift with the main current for thousands of miles. Eventually the North American type reach the⁺ American coast. They grow and develop into elvers, which are young eels, and travel to estuaries and freshwater rivers. They stay there for several years feeding and grow-ing to adults. When they are nearly ready to breed again the skin becomes silvery and the eyes enlarge. They now begin their journey to the breeding grounds, which are thought to be in the Sargasso Sea. They spawn in spring, and later the larvae hatch out. Thus the cycle is complete. European eel larvae are carried to Europe and to the Mediterranean Sea where they find freshwater before returning to the sea as adults.

Left The pattern of eel migration in the Atlantic.

Migration of turtles, whales and birds

Some animals, including seals, whales, birds and turtles may also travel long distances. Seals spend much of their life in the water, but breed on shore. The large baleen whales live in warm, tropical seas in the winter months. Here they mate and later give birth to their calves. In spring they swim over 3,200 kilometres (2,000 miles) to the cold polar seas, where they feed during the summer months on the swarms of small, shrimp-like animals which live in these cold waters. The whales build up a thick layer of fat (blubber) under their skin. In the autumn they swim back again to warmer waters. Sperm whales and some of the smaller dolphins also travel great distances, but their movements are not so regular as the yearly migrations of baleen whales.

Some birds fly many thousands of miles over the sea. Arctic terns breed in the summer on lands near the Arctic Ocean, on river banks, sand banks or tidelines. Later in the year they fly south towards Africa, and many spend the winter in the Antarctic. In contrast, the great shearwater breeds in the South Atlantic on an island called Tristan da Cunha, and after breeding it migrates northwards.

The green turtle lives in warm, shallow water mainly in the Caribbean, off Mexico, Brazil and Africa. On feeding grounds there the turtles live on turtle-grass. Breeding occurs every two or three years. At those times the turtles migrate to nesting sites which may be

Below A whaling ship with its catch. Today many kinds of whale are protected.

many kilometres away. One group is thought to travel over 1,600 kilometres (1,000 miles) from the coast of Brazil to Ascension Island. They mate together in the water. At the nesting sites, the females go ashore several times to lay eggs. They then return to the feeding grounds. When the baby turtles hatch out they head for the sea. Many are picked off by hunting seabirds, but those that make it to the water are carried by currents to the feeding grounds.

Above Green turtle hatchlings emerge from their nest in the sand to make the perilous journey to the sea. Female turtles often lay several dozen eggs at a time.

8 LIFE ON THE SEA SHORES

Life at the tideline

The sea shore is a frontier between the land and the sea. Animals and plants which live between the tidemarks are called 'intertidal'. They must be able to withstand the regular exposure to wind and sun as they are uncovered when the tide goes out twice each day. They must also be able to resist the pounding of the waves breaking on them when the tide is in. Seaweeds of the shore usually have thick and leathery 'fronds' which prevent the plants from drying out at low tide, but bend without breaking in the violent water movements at high tide. Many intertidal animals, such as the limpet, clamp themselves firmly on to the rocks at low tide, and move about only when they are covered by water. Others, such as crabs, shelter during low tide under masses of damp weed or rock. Yet others, such as many worms and cockles, burrow beneath the sand or mud. Finally, many of these animals avoid the effects of low tide by living in rock pools, where they remain until the tide comes in again.

Each type (or species) of animal and plant on the shore occupies a particular area or 'zone', depending on how well it can stand exposure to the drying effects of the sun and the wind. This 'zonation' is most obvious on steep, rocky shores. Here, if we take a close look, we are able to see distinct bands of colour or texture. A black, red or very dark grey band at the top of the shore is produced by a lichen covering

Above A thick-lipped grey mullet stranded in a pool with a prawn. It eats mud and algae, worms and crustaceans.

Above Beutiful red-and-white dahlia sea anemones with their tentacles extended to catch food.

the rocks. Below this, nearer the sea, there is often a much lighter band produced by the shells of millions of barnacles cemented to the rock surface. Lower still can be seen bands of yellow, brown or olive-green. These are caused by layers of different seaweeds. Finally, during very low spring tides, large kelp may be seen.

Right Life in a rock pool. Dog whelks feed on edible mussels and acorn barnacles. You can also see beadlet anemones and limpets.

Sea birds and seals

Stretching from the Arctic in the north to the Antarctic in the south, the Atlantic Ocean spans both the coldest and the warmest regions of the world. We may find sea birds such as puffins or cormorants, and seals like the grey seal, in some temperate zones. However, sea birds and seals much prefer the colder zones in the far north and south. We could travel for days through the tropics without seeing either, but we could see hundreds or thousands of seals and sea birds on the shores of an Arctic or Antarctic island in summer.

Both birds and seals are well adapted for coping with cold. They carry a thick layer of fat under the skin, which helps keep them warm and gives them a reserve of energy. The birds have dense, waterproof plumage (feathers), and some seals have thick fur. Others rely completely on their thick skin and fat to keep the cold out. So long as they can feed well, they can keep warm.

On an island like South Georgia, far south in the Atlantic Ocean, there will be huge elephant seals and smaller fur seals breeding on the beaches in groups so large and numerous that it would be difficult to pick your way among them. Look out to sea, and there will almost certainly be a leopard seal coasting up and down, hoping to catch a penguin or two for dinner.

On some beaches we might see stately king penguins with their orange shoulder flashes, and smaller gentoo and macaroni penguins. There will be brown skuas hunting for abandoned eggs in the penguin colonies, Dominican gulls and little white sheathbills scavenging on the beaches. On the slopes above may be three or four nesting species of albatross, and deep among the roots of the tussock grass, several species of burrowing sea birds that come out only at night.

Left An aggressive bull elephant seal.

Above right A pair of wandering albatross.

Below right A puffin coming in to land.

46

9 A VISIT TO SOME ISLANDS

The Azores

Most of the islands in the Atlantic Ocean are of volcanic origin – that is, they were made by underwater volcanoes which gradually grew until they rose above sea-level. The Azores are no exception, and they contain many active volcanoes. However, this does not make the islands barren or uninteresting. The climate is warm, and moist sea air rising over the volcanic mountains produces plenty of rain, so vegetation flourishes. During the summer the islands are covered with beautiful hydrangeas. One island is so full of flowers that it was named Flores, which means 'flowers' in Portuguese, the language of the people who live there.

Farming and fishing are both very important on the Azores. Cattle thrive in the green fields, and fruit and vegetables are grown. One speciality is pineapples, which are grown in greenhouses. Most of the towns and villages are on the coasts, away from the mountains inland. These are natural centres for fishing, and in the past there was also a strong whaling industry here. Now, unfortunately, whales have been hunted so much that they are rarely seen around the Azores.

Until recently, the islanders have lived largely by their agriculture and fishing – exporting food to Europe in return for cars, machinery and other goods. But light industries and the tourist trade are beginning to be more important. The islanders are also hoping to use their volcanoes to generate electricity. To do this, they are drilling holes deep into the earth's crust. Far below the surface there is hot steam, produced when rainwater, sinking down through cracks in the ground, meets the hot rocks deep inside the volcanoes. The steam can be piped to the surface and used to drive generators. Using this 'geothermal' power, the people of the Azores will be able to manufacture many more things themselves.

Left Sao Miguel, Azores. A windmill on the edge of the village of Remedios overlooking the sea.

Right Harvesting tea on Sao Miguel, Azores.

The Canary and Cape Verde Islands

Off the coast of north-west Africa lie the hot, sun-baked Canary Islands. There are seven main islands and many smaller ones, all formed by volcanic action. Though mostly inactive now, several of the islands still have hot rocks and recent lava flows, and look as though they were formed fairly recently. The largest island, Tenerife, has a magnificent volcanic peak 3,718 metres (12,198 ft) high. It forms a landmark that can be seen from a long way away. La Palma, one of the smaller western islands, has a volcanic crater ten kilometres (6 miles) across with a rim that rises over 2,400 metres (almost 8,000 ft) above sea-level. There is black and red volcanic sand on the beaches. The eastern islands, Lanzarote and Fuerteventura, are still dotted with volcanic cones and lava flows.

Named originally by the Romans from the big dogs *(canes)* that ran wild on the islands, the Canaries in turn gave their name to the bright yellow finches that sing in their woodlands, and have become popular as cage-birds. The Canaries were occupied originally by Africans, but were conquered by Spanish colonists during the fifteenth century and have remained Spanish possessions. Today, over a million people live on the Canary Islands. They make a living from fishing and farming. They grow tobacco, bananas, sugar, tropical fruits and vegetables. Recently, the islands have become a tourist attraction.

Further south, off the bulge of Africa, lie the

Below A farmer ploughing up the black volcanic soil with 'camel power' on Lanzarote, Canary Islands.

scattered Cape Verde Islands. There are ten large islands and five smaller ones. The total population is just over a quarter of a million. Like the Canaries, these are volcanic islands. The main harbour of Sao Vicente is an extinct crater, and the tallest mountain is an active volcano rising to 2,800 metres (9,281 ft). The Cape Verdes are hotter and drier than the Canary Islands, and crops can only be grown in the damp atmosphere of the uplands and valleys. People who live along the coast rely mainly on fishing for a living, and the islands export a good deal of canned fish.

Right Lava formation on Tenerife with Mount Teide in the background.

Below A banana plantation on Tenerife. Bananas are an important commercial crop.

51

Ascension Island, St Helena

Further south again, almost half-way between Africa and South America, lies the lonely island of Ascension. Only eleven kilometres (7 miles) across, it is made up mostly of dry lava plains and cinder cones, which are reminders of its volcanic origins. The main mountain, Green Mountain, rises to 875 metres (2,870 ft). It is capped with vegetation – mostly trees and

Below Pasture land in the hills of St Helena, which lies to the south of Ascension Island.

shrubs brought in from other parts of the world, for it had none of its own when it was first discovered in the early sixteenth century. Ascension remained uninhabited until 1815, when a British Royal Navy garrison was put ashore. Since then it has been occupied continuously by the British. Later in the nineteenth century, the island was used as a linking point for submarine cables. During the Second World War an important airstrip was built there, and since then it has become a

communications centre. There are no native inhabitants, but about 1,000 Britons, Americans and St Helenians live there. These people are mostly radio engineers and technicians and their families. The main centre, Georgetown, has a small school and hospital, and Green Mountain is farmed to provide fresh meat and vegetables for the inhabitants.

Over 1,000 kilometres (600 miles) south-east of Ascension lies St Helena, another tiny volcanic island of the tropical Atlantic. St Helena has a long-established population. These people are mainly descendants of East Indian and African slaves who once worked the plantations there. About 5,000 of them live on its 122 square kilometres (76 sq miles) of green, rolling uplands.

Historically, the island is important as the place where Napoleon was kept in exile from 1815 to his death in 1821. St Helena has been maintained as a British colony ever since. It is a poor island, for only about one-third of the land is farmed, and there is little else to provide its population with a living.

Below A view towards the sea across tropical vegetation and volcanic mountain ranges on Ascension Island.

10 HOW THE SEA CAN HELP US

Resources of the continental shelf

Many of the sea's resources – that is, the products which are useful to us – are found on the continental shelves. These are just extensions of the continents which are covered by a shallow layer of water. During the Ice Age a few hundred thousand years ago, when much of the water was locked up as ice in glaciers on land, many continental shelves were uncovered – much of the North Sea and English Channel for example. Minerals found underground may also be found under the continental shelves. For example, coal is found in England and also under the North Sea.

Much of the oil and gas which we now use comes from the continental shelves off Europe, America and Africa. To recover oil, special 'drilling platforms' which float in the sea are used to sink pipes into the underground rocks containing the oil. When oil is found, it is brought to the surface through enormous structures called 'production platforms' which actually stand on the sea-bed. They are used to control the flow of oil. The oil is piped ashore along the bottom of the sea. Building and working on production platforms and pipelines at sea is difficult. Divers have to be employed to check and repair the underwater structures. Some structures are so deep that the divers have to work in diving bells or even miniature submarines called 'submersibles'.

Above A ship takes supplies to an oil rig. The oil will be piped ashore along the sea-bed.

It is important to make sure that oil does not escape into the sea, otherwise the water will become polluted. If that happens, fish and birds may be killed, and beaches spoiled. The sea can become polluted in other ways too: for example, when factories carelessly allow poisonous waste products to be discharged into rivers which flow into the sea. As we come to use the oceans more and more, we must also be more careful to look after them.

Right Divers working on oil rigs face difficult conditions. The water may be stormy or bitterly cold.

Below The supertanker, *Amoco Cadiz*, is broken up by heavy seas off the coast of Brittany. Most of her oil was spilt into the sea.

Fishing

Many of the commercial fish (that is, fish that are caught for food in large quantities) live in the waters over the continental shelves. Here there is plenty of food (plankton for example) for them to eat. The annual catch of all the Atlantic nations is about 25 million tonnes. This does not include the fish caught in the Atlantic by Japan, Korea, Italy, Romania and other non-Atlantic countries. The annual total catch of all the countries in the world is only 75 million tonnes, so you can see that Atlantic fisheries are very important.

Much of the fish in the North Atlantic is found in the cold water around Europe, Canada, Iceland and Norway. Here cod, plaice, haddock and coley are caught, usually by specially designed trawlers. Once herring was important but now it has become scarce because it has been overfished. In the warmer water, a little nearer the equator, there are sardines, mackerel and tuna fish. There, instead of the varieties of crabs and lobsters found in the north, we find spiny lobsters and prawns. Around countries near the equator, all kinds of fish are caught, often by men in canoes. To the west, in the Gulf of Mexico and along the north coast of South America, shrimps are trawled. Off Argentina, Brazil and south-west Africa there are hake fisheries.

Above A spiny lobster from the north-east Atlantic. It can grow to 50cm and is very good to eat.

In the past, fishermen of one country have been able to fish quite close to the coast of other countries around the Atlantic as well as in the open sea. However, since 1976 most countries have increased their fishing limits from only five kilometres (3 miles) to 320 kilometres (200 miles), which often includes the rich fisheries of the continental shelf area. Now trawlers have difficulty in finding fishing grounds outside their own country's territory.

Not all fish caught are used for human food. Some, such as anchovy, capelin, sprats and blue whiting are made into fish-meal, and given to animals to increase the protein in their diet.

Left Sorting the catch on a fishing boat at Mar del Plata, Argentina. The fish will be mainly croaker, hawkfish, mackerel and a few anchovy.

57

Other resources

Many other useful materials can be recovered from the sea-bed, of which one of the most important is gravel. On the continental shelves, sand and silt can settle where the currents are gentle; but in areas of strong currents small particles are swept away and only large pebbles are left. These form gravel, which is valuable for making concrete. Countries such as Britain, France and the United States obtain gravel from their continental shelves.

The gravel is recovered by dredging – that is, scooping it off the sea-bed with a specially designed machine. This must be done with care, however, for removing large amounts of sea-floor material may cause currents to flow differently, and then sediments might be eroded (worn away) or deposited in different places. This could be unfortunate if, for example, it caused sediment to pile up near the entrance to a harbour. So special studies are made before large-scale dredging takes place, to check whether there would be any unwanted effects.

As we find out more about the deep sea, we find that useful resources may be found in the ocean basins themselves, and not only on the continental shelves. It is now expected that oil may be found in some of the thick sediments near the foot of the continental slope (that is,

the steep slope at the edge of the continental shelf). Other minerals can be found farther from land – for example in 'manganese nodules'. These are lumps of material lying on top of the sediments of the deep ocean floor. They contain valuable metals such as manganese, nickel and copper. They range in size from pebbles to small boulders. It is thought that they too could be recovered by dredging, but one problem that remains unsolved is who they would belong to. Legally, no country owns any ocean beyond certain limits from its shores. Probably the fairest solution would be to share the resources of the deep sea among all the countries of the world.

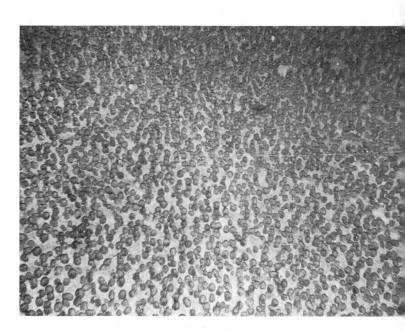

Above Manganese nodules are found on the deep sea floor. In the future it should be possible to extract chemicals from them.

Left This gravel dredger is at work off the west coast of Britain.

11 PORTS AND SHIPS

Life at ports

There are many hundreds of ports on the coastline of the Atlantic Ocean. They vary in many ways, but all have the same basic purpose. As a junction between land and sea, all ports provide a place where goods or people can be unloaded from, or loaded on to ships, so that trade may take place. Without trade the products of other countries would not reach our shops.

As new and larger ships are built, and as trade changes, ports have to develop. Manhattan Island, the original port of New York, is a good example. Starting as a small Dutch colony, New York grew gradually as Europeans arrived there from the eighteenth century onwards, and trade links were established inland and across the ocean. In order that this trade could take place as quickly and profitably as possible, the government and richer merchants provided certain facilities. These included wharfs and docks, roads and railways, warehouses and cranes. They also included the people who provided services, such as dockers, customs officers, ship-repairers and lifeboatmen.

As a port, New York was ideally sited. Manhattan Island, and the smaller islands round it, provided over 1,120 kilometres (700 miles) of waterfront, the channels were deep, and the small tidal changes allowed docking throughout the day. Other industries also flourished in New York. Many of these bene-

Above A tug accompanies a cargo boat into Manhattan harbour. You can see the skyscrapers of New York towering in the background.

Right Ships at dock in Buenos Aires, an important port in Argentina.

fited from being at the port because they used goods brought in by ships. These 'port industries', such as oil-refining, iron-smelting and flour-milling can be found at many ports throughout the world.

Today, however, New York is overcrowded. Manhattan Island is small and surrounded by rivers which must be bridged. The great passenger liners are disappearing with the growth of air transport. The largest 'supertankers' cannot use the harbour. New ports have been built on the mainland, and in particular an important new 'container' depot has been built south of the city. Here, a good deal of cargo is loaded from huge trucks on to ships in vast containers, and unloaded from incoming ships into the depots, where trucks are waiting to take the goods to factories and offices.

Shipping

Transportation across the North Atlantic Ocean became famous in the last quarter of the nineteenth century, when luxury passenger liners from many nations competed with each other for the fastest crossing between Europe and New York. The last ship to hold the speed record was the American-owned liner *United States*, which reclaimed it from the *Queen Mary* in 1952 with a speed of over 35 knots (65 k.p.h.).

The most famous liner ever to sail from Southampton for New York was the ill-fated *Titanic*. The disastrous outcome of that voyage, with the sinking of the *Titanic*, has had a lasting effect on all the merchant fleets throughout the world. The *Titanic* did not have enough lifeboats to cater for all its passengers, and so many lives were lost. As a result, international laws governing safety at sea have been laid down. These state that all ships should carry more than enough life-saving equipment to enable all passengers and crew to be saved in the event of an emergency.

The traffic between Europe and the United States continued for many years after the *Titanic* disaster, but with the introduction of cheaper and faster air travel during the Sixties, these great passenger vessels began to be less popular. Many were laid up. The *United States* and *America* were laid up near Norfolk, Virginia, and many other European-owned vessels were scrapped or sold to owners in the Far East. Two famous British-owned ships ended their lives rather differently. The *Queen Elizabeth* was sold to Hong Kong interests, and after catching fire in Hong Kong harbour, was declared a total loss. The *Queen Mary* ended her life as a floating museum in Long Beach, California. One remaining luxury liner which still sails regularly between Europe and the United States is the *Queen Elizabeth II* (QE2).

The fastest ships which now sail between the two continents are container ships. These steam at up to 30 knots. Although they waste a certain amount of hold space by keeping their cargo in containers, this disadvantage is outweighed by the great ease of loading and unloading, and the better protection this system gives goods while at sea. All vessels sailing from Europe to the Americas use the 'great circle' course, which was the original course taken by the *Titanic* although she did steam further north in an attempt to reach the United States faster.

The North Atlantic is also a place where many of the major naval fleets practise manoeuvres. The NATO fleets carry out most of their exercises in this area.

Above right An armada of small craft escort the *Queen Mary* on her last voyage to Long Beach, California, where she has been converted into a museum.

Below right Stormy seas sweep the decks of an oil tanker crossing the Atlantic in the half light of dusk.

12 HOW SCIENTISTS STUDY THE AREA

Submersibles and cameras

It is very difficult to see underwater. If we were able to stand on top of a great underwater mountain, we would see only a few metres down the slope into the water. However, light is used to illuminate and record the animals in the sea, and the form of the rocks and sediments on the sea floor.

In the Atlantic, where the ocean is usually four to five kilometres (2 to 3 miles) deep, scientists lower cameras and lights on long ropes from research ships so that they can take photographs. Specially strong cameras have been designed which are able to withstand the enormous pressure of the deep water. These will take photographs as the ship drifts on the surface. In this way, scientists have been able to study some of the animals that live in the deep ocean, and also the nature and form of the sea floor. One of the most recent and most exciting ways of using such cameras is to fix them to a towed sledge net which catches the animals living near the bottom. As the sledge is towed along by the ship above, the camera and flash unit are timed to take photographs every few minutes. In this way biologists see the animals that are in the path of the sledge nets and also record rocks and sediment on the ocean floor.

Another way to see what is happening in the depths of the ocean is to go down in a small research submersible, such as the American *Alvin* or the French-made *Trieste*. Submersibles like these have a steel or titanium sphere in which two men can sit, protected from the pressure outside. One man is the pilot, who controls the propulsion motors and depth of the submersible, while the other observes, takes photographs and operates the scientific instruments on board. In 1974, the French and Americans co-operated in making dives like these on the Mid-Atlantic Ridge, the mountains which form the 'backbone' of the Atlantic (see p. 12). A great deal was learned about the central valley in the mountains where new ocean-floor material is produced.

Below 'Jim', a one-man, super diving suit/submersible, which allows maintenance and other work to be carried out safely in deep water.

Above This submersible, *Mantis*, is used for all kinds of underwater research.

Other instruments

Although neither people nor cameras can see far in the oceans, there is something which can. That is 'sound'. Sound (acoustic) waves can be made to travel thousands of kilometres if the frequency is right. Whales use sound to communicate and find their way over great distances.

Scientists use acoustic instruments regularly to do a variety of tasks. Echo-sounders are used to measure the depth of the ocean; instruments called 'sonars' are used to detect fish and 'view' the sea floor; and sound is also used to position research ships accurately and to pass information from instruments suspended in a net or mounted on the sea floor to the surface. Sound underwater helps to replace the sight we use on land, and if we wish to 'see' the panoramas which lie so far down, we have to use sound instead of our eyes. An instrument called 'Gloria' has recently been developed which can 'see' the mountains and valleys on the ocean floor up to a range of 24 kilometres (15 miles) either side of a research ship.

Many other types of instruments are used by chemists, physicists, biologists and geologists, as they study the oceans. These include special 'water bottles' for collecting water samples. There are also 'floats' which have weights so that they stay at a particular depth in the ocean and then can be tracked as they drift with the water masses around the oceans of the world. And there are nets for catching animals which can be made to open or close by

Above A scientist on board ship checks a graph of the sea and sea floor produced by an echo-sounder.

remote control at any time, so that a catch can be taken at a known depth.

There are also very precise electronic instruments which will measure the temperature and the saltiness of the sea at different depths. Geologists need to know the nature of the sediments and rocks of the ocean floor, so there are instruments designed to take samples of these sediments, and others to dredge up the rocks.

We have only just begun to explore the deepest parts of the oceans. During the coming years, different and more advanced instruments will be developed which will help us find out more about the mysteries of the sea.

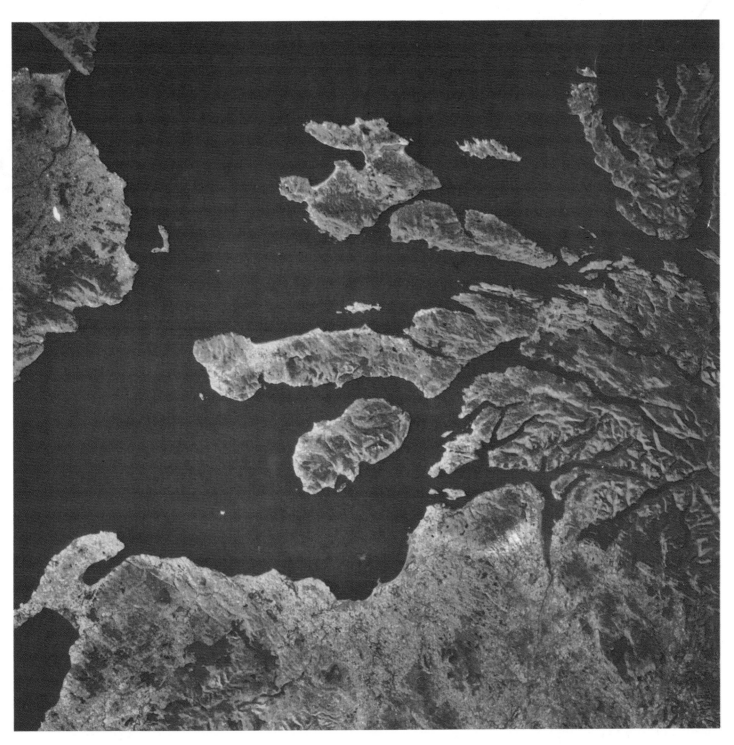

Above A satellite picture of the north-west coast of Scotland. Such pictures can tell us a good deal about the land and the sea.

Glossary

Barnacle A small shellfish which clings to rocks and the bottoms of ships

Carnivore An animal which eats other animals. A shark is a carnivore.

Container ships Fast cargo boats which carry their goods packed in large containers rather than loose.

Continental drift The movement of the landmasses of the world towards or away from each other.

Continental shelf That part of a continent which lies off-shore and is covered by a shallow layer of water.

Continental slope The slope joining the end of the continental shelf to the deeper part of the ocean.

Crustacean Animal (usually living in the sea) with a hard shell and many legs. Prawns, crabs and lobsters are all crustaceans.

Current The flow of water in a given direction.

Echo-sounder Instrument which uses sound to measure the depth of the ocean.

Equator An imaginary line making a circle round the earth halfway between the North and South Poles.

Estuary The wide, open mouth of a river, where it joins the sea.

Fossil The remains, impression or trace of an animal or plant found preserved in a rock.

Geothermal power Energy obtained in the form of hot water or high-pressure steam from hot areas below the earth's surface.

Glacier A huge mass of ice that moves extremely slowly down a mountainside.

Herbivore An animal which eats plants rather than the flesh of other animals.

Ice Age Period of pre-history when a large part of the earth's surface was covered with ice.

Iceberg A large mass of ice floating in the colder seas.

Icelandic sagas Epic poems dating from the eleventh to the thirteenth centuries. They are almost our only source of knowledge about the ancient Scandinavian peoples.

Kelp The biggest seaweeds. Found below the low-water mark and growing up to a depth of 30 metres (100 ft) below sea-level.

Limpet A small shellfish which clings to rocks.

Manganese nodules Lumps of valuable metals (e.g. manganese, nickel and copper) found on the ocean floor.

Mid-Atlantic Ridge Range of underwater mountains in the centre of the Atlantic.

Migration Regular movement of fish, animals or birds from one region to another for feeding, breeding or to find a warmer climate.

Mineral Any substance in the earth or under the sea-bed which can be dug out and used. Coal, iron ore and gold are minerals.

Mollusc A soft animal without a backbone, such as an octopus or a squid. Some (mussels, snails, whelks) have a protective shell.

NATO North Atlantic Treaty Organization. A military alliance (1949) of the U.S.A., Canada and European countries to defend members against the U.S.S.R. and its allies.

Neap tide Small tide occurring when the Sun and Moon are pulling against each other.

Plankton Tiny animals (zooplankton) and plants (phytoplankton) which drift in millions through the seas.

Pollution Contamination of sea-water by dangerous chemicals from industry, oil spillage and sewage or other rubbish.

Salinity Saltiness. The salinity of sea-water varies a little according to the depth of the water and its distance from the Poles.

Sediments Clay, sand and silt which collects on the sea floor and may become hard rocks. Remains of dead animals are also incorporated into the sediments.

Silt Fine sand and fertile soil washed down to the sea by rivers.

Sonar Instrument used to detect fish and explore the

sea floor by sound waves.

Spawn To produce a cluster of eggs.

Spring tide Exceptionally high and low tides occurring about once a fortnight when the Sun and Moon pull together.

Submersible A small research submarine used for observing life in the ocean depths.

Tides The rise and fall of sea-level which usually occurs twice a day because of the attraction of the Sun and Moon.

Tropics Hot countries which are found on either side of two imaginary circles at equal distances north and south of the equator.

Twilight zone The dimly lit region of the ocean from about 200 to 800 metres below sea-level. There is not enough light here for plants to grow.

Below Heavy seas can cause problems for sailors. Here a lifeboat tows a yacht to safety during the recent Fastnet race off the south coast of Ireland.

The people who wrote this book

Pat Hargreaves   Marine biologist, Institute of Oceanographic Sciences, Surrey.

Dr Roger Searle   Marine geophysicist, Institute of Oceanographic Sciences, Surrey.

Margaret B. Deacon   Visiting Fellow, Institute for Advanced Studies in the Humanities, University of Edinburgh.

Dr W. John Gould   Marine Physicist, Institute of Oceanographic Sciences, Surrey.

Laurence Draper   Marine Physicist, Institute of Oceanographic Sciences, Surrey.

Dr David Pugh   Marine Physicist, Institute of Oceanographic Sciences, Merseyside.

Dr A. Rice   Marine biologist, Institute of Oceanographic Sciences, Surrey.

Dr Sidney G. Brown   Marine Zoologist, Sea Mammal Research Unit, British Antarctic Survey, Cambridge.

Dr Bernard Stonehouse   Biologist and specialist in marine birds and animals, Senior Lecturer, University of Bradford.

H. S. Noel   Journalist in fisheries and marine subjects.

S. C. Pitcher   Teacher of geography, King's College School, London.

Alan Thorpe   Editor, *Shipping World*, London.

Dr S. Rusby   Marine physicist, Institute of Oceanographic Sciences, Surrey.

Index

Books to read

Angel, M. and H., *Ocean Life* (Octopus Books)
Cochrane, J., *The Amazing World of the Sea* (Angus & Robertson)
Keeling, C. H., *Under the Sea* (F. Watts)
Lambert, D., *The Oceans* (Ward Lock)
McMillan, N. F., *The Observer's Book of Seashells of the British Isles* (F. Warne)
Merret, N., *The How and Why Wonder Book of the Deep Sea* (Transworld)
Parsons, J., *Oceans* (Macdonald Educational)
Stonehouse, B., *The Living World of the Sea* (Hamlyn)

Picture acknowledgements

Michael Allman and Blandford Press 16; Heather Angel 39, 45 (*above*); Biofoto 35 (*below*); Allan Cash 6, 49, 51 (*both*), 63 (*below*); Bruce Coleman, by the following photographers: Mack Boulton 32–3; Jane Burton 37 (*both*), 38, 41, 44, 45; Inigo Everson 56; M. P. Harris 47; D. & K. Urry 47; Dr Frieder Saner 34; Robert Schroeder 43; Bill Wood 36; Energy Technology Support Unit 29 (*above*); D. P. Wilson/Eric and David Hosking 35 (*above*), 46, 57; Alan Hutchison 60, front cover; Institute of Oceanographic Sciences 17, 25, 59, 66; Anna Jupp 10–11, 13, 24, 30, 40, back cover; Keystone Press 55 (*below*); Mansell 19, 20, 21, 27 (*right*); Marex Ltd 27 (*left*); John Mitchell 12, 26; Nigel Press Associates 67; Oceaneering International Services Ltd 64; Offshore Systems Engineering Ltd 65; Popperfoto 18, 69; Seaphot 48, 50, 58; Bernard Stonehouse 52, 53; John Topham 8–9, 28, 29 (*below*), 31, 42; U.S. Travel Service 63 (*above*); Wayland Picture Library 22–3, 54, 55; Zefa 14, 61, title page.